THE
HEIST

Escaping A Narcissist: The Blueprint

JEMEICA P. FRECKLETON

ISBN: 979-8-5555215-0-7

DEDICATION

God indeed takes his time when putting together a plan, especially when it involves one of His own. He has precisely and intricately woven every detail, every incident, every encounter, and every meeting, to produce the final product you see today. It is by no chance that any of our paths have crossed.

This book is for anyone to read who has had similar experiences with a narcissist and was too afraid to speak or stand up for themselves. This book is also for those still battling and working through traumatic experiences or abuse of any form. Know that I have made your struggle a personal matter and will not stop bringing awareness to the issue of narcissism and domestic violence.

To the woman who inspired the idea behind this book, Rhondi Forbes, know that you are the reason it was written. I remember our conversation vividly! And, as promised, this is your dedication. Consider this a very belated birthday gift. You brought to life something that I thought I had buried. You gave me hope again when I felt like I had none. For once, I did not feel "crazy" because you could relate to my experiences, as we had a mutual abuser. Hearing your story gave me the courage to tell mine and become a voice for you and every other female! Know that you are kind, brave, and stronger than you, yourself, know. I am glad that I met you.

To those who believed in me, always supported me, encouraged me, and gave this project the green light, I want to say a huge thank you. This includes my family members and close friends, who are far too many to mention, but you definitely know who you are. Thank you for being such an important piece of my story.

A special thank you to my parents, Brenda Freckleton and James Freckleton, also my brother Najee Freckleton. You all are my backbone for every project or new endeavor that I pursue. You have always allowed me to fully express myself, and for that, I am grateful. I have always had your support in all the good times and the bad times. Thank you for making me believe that I can do anything and everything in life.

ACKNOWLEDGEMENTS

This book also would not have been possible without these key and most valuable players:

To Brooke & Lee Co. and Britney Seymour, my publisher and editor: This would not have been possible without your willingness to take on this project, clean it up and make my words make sense. You allowed me to take my emotions and channel them to an audience. Thank you.

Nadia and Rodney Bain: My cousins, who played a pivotal role in the editing process. When I pitched The Heist, you were sold from the introduction. To work along with someone that believes, just as much as you do, in your project is a powerful thing.

I doubted the idea of writing a book, then I thought about the great authors who came before me. You are my source of inspiration:

Ashanti Marshall. Thank you for sharing your resources and experiences. You have been a blessing to me. I intend to do the same for others who seek to write a book but, like me, initially did not know where to begin.

Gilberta Thompson: Without hesitation, you began breaking down the steps and provided me a detailed outline for what I wanted to address in this project. Your last blog about 'The Parable of The Gifts' was the icing on the cake for me. I could not forgive myself if I ignored that sign. Now, look at my gift making room for little old me.

Carmell Laing: What began as me needing guidance on a fast quickly led to you becoming one of my sources for wise counsel and a spiritual advisor. What would be my hardest relationship would soon prove to be my greatest triumph and the beginning of a purposeful journey. You played a major role in this. I thank you for answering my calls, voice notes and messages, no matter the hour. Thank you for your advice. Above all, I thank you for allowing me to realize that everything I needed, God had already placed in me!

God: All honor and glory be to You. When You told me You had this handled, I should have given it to You a long time ago. I wanted people to know what I went through. I wanted to tell my side of the story, but You begged me to be patient. I thank You for the insight and for connecting me to the right, like-minded people. I thank You for the revelation and for every intentional path taken that led to this day. You are my ultimate source of joy and peace. I thank You for revealing to me that real validation only comes from You. I thank You for allowing me to go through everything I did to shape this message and for it to be shared at the appointed time. No one can ever stop what You intended for good.

Table of Contents

INTRODUCTION

The powerful thing about perspective is that it challenges you to see the world from a vantage point other than your own. A prime example of this is reflected in a photo I saw circulating on a social media platform. This photo showed two people sitting on a bus. The person who sat on the left side of the bus enjoyed vibrant greenery and scenic views. Meanwhile, the person who sat on the right side of the bus observed rocks on the unimpressive mountainous side. Let it be known that there were only two passengers on the bus. The person who appeared to have a dismal view could have changed their seat for a better view, or simply look to the right, but he didn't. Dr. Wayner Dyer, a world-renowned author and motivational speaker, summarized perspective best, "If we change the way we look at things, the things we look at change."

Maybe you're thinking, "Why would you name a book The Heist?" Doesn't the main character share her personal triumphs? Well, I know it sounds odd, but then again, it's all a matter of perspective. By definition, a heist is a robbery; it indicates that something was taken unlawfully. Now, let's change the dynamics. Would you consider stealing something if it had great value to you?

Think about it, if you were in a desperate situation, would you make a deal to steal something if it meant that you would receive, let's say, one million dollars? No? Well, the truth is, I probably wouldn't either, so let's go ahead and up the ante. Would you conduct a heist if it were to get a loved one who had been kidnapped back? Let's say it's your mother, or your spouse, or maybe even your child? I think I've tugged on your heartstrings a little, and now your perspective has shifted. Admit it, you stopped for a second to consider it, didn't you? Now, what if I made it more personal? What if the ultimate goal of the heist was to get back your most prized possession...Your life? What about your joy? How about your self-esteem? Maybe your worth? Possibly, your peace of mind? Even your name? I think by now, some of you have been officially recruited, but for the remainder of you who may need a little more convincing, stick with me and I will share with you the blueprint. Now that I have your complete and undivided attention... Ladies and gentlemen, welcome to the greatest heist ever seen in history.

PART ONE

THE BLUEPRINT

"...The success of a heist mostly
depends on a well-developed
action plan. "

Chapter 1

THE PLOT

A heist involves extensive planning and preparation. Some heists take years to develop before they are actually executed. *The Millennium Dome Raid*: A group of robbers planned an explosion and entered firing guns; they escaped with a diamond. These guys were already under surveillance and had been arrested on site. Lesson 1: Timing is everything. *The Collar Bomb Bank Robbery*: This guy was actually a ploy, or an accessory, in a heist. He escaped with the money, but he was later caught and even admitted to being forced to wear a bomb. The bomb detonated. Lesson 2: If you have nothing to gain from the heist, you may jeopardize the entire plan. *The Great Train Robbery*: The robbers got away with money, then played a game of monopoly in an abandoned building, leaving a trail of evidence behind, even fingerprints; they, too, were all caught. Lesson 3: Never get too relaxed or complacent; always remain on guard, even when you got what you needed from the heist. All of these heists had the potential to be successful; they obtained the prize, had it in hand, and escaped, but ultimately did not elude capture. Despite being well planned and properly executed, history has deemed these heists unsuccessful. Essentially, they were all caught, not because of a lack of preparation, but because they were either too eager, too fearful, or too distracted.

Hi, allow me to introduce myself, we don't know each other personally, but we are all linked by one common factor. We all lost something quite immoderate, and today, I am the person who is going to help you get it back. Close your eyes and think for a moment about the last time you were free; think about the last time you were genuinely happy. Now that you have that moment on your big screen, pause that image! That's your momentum; whenever you feel like backing out or aborting this mission, that is your drive.

There is a criminal on the loose and while there have been no formal accusations made by the proper authority, his rap sheet is extensive and growing. The criminal charges brought against his perpetrator are as follows and not limited to: Accessory to murder, assault & battery, aggravated assault, attempted burglary, kidnapping, manslaughter; involuntary and voluntary probation violation, perjury, cyberbullying, disorderly conduct, conspiracy, stalking, fraud, theft, hate crimes, identity theft, forgery, harassment, embezzlement, prostitution, robbery, racketeering and domestic violence. While they wait to decide whether or not to pursue this case, I have deemed him armed and extremely dangerous. Approach with great caution.

Clearly, this is not his first robbery. So he is well aware of our playbook, and because of this, he is always one step ahead. He is extremely cunning and intelligent. He is meticulous and well organized, so that means there is little room for error on our part. We must be prepared at all times because he will attempt to blindside you. In the game of Chess, remember your aim is to think of your player's next move.

The success of a heist mostly depends on a well-developed action plan. We have already discussed the who and our why, now let us address the how. A brilliant execution occurs through clear communication and understanding; we must become fully aware and knowledgeable about our target as we implement and utilize specific tools. By monitoring the target and the circumstances surrounding it, we ensure that everything is going as planned. We should make note of and verbalize any changes noticed. Remember the goal and stay focused on the prize the entire time. We can achieve our goal by identifying corrective measures to get back or remain on track; we may consider employing additional time, phases and/ or resources as we deem necessary.

Let me remind you, although I may have orchestrated the heist, everything that's required is already within you. You just need a structured plan, the tools, and a team to make this heist a success. You've been chosen because of your expertise; who better than the person who has encountered an individual with a similar profile. I will make it my mission to ensure we ALL get out alive. Now, let the heist begin!

Chapter 2

THE PROFILES

The reason why a perpetrator selects a victim varies. Qualities that are perceived as desirable serve as a motivation for victimizing. Availability, opportunities, characteristics and vulnerability are all key determining factors. Understanding these motives provides valuable insight and can narrow the focus of an investigation. A particular pattern or technique commonly utilized can easily identify an unknown or known perpetrator, or even similar persons that fit the description. The more information gathered from a crime scene, the more accurately a criminal profile can be built. This data ensures that the one who committed the offense is successfully caught.

Let's meet the narcissist, also known as the perpetrator. This is a person who has a personality disorder that results in an inflated or exaggerated sense of their own importance; he/ she continually craves attention and admiration. A narcissist generally lacks empathy and possesses other dysfunctional attitudes and behavior. At first glance, they appear to be convincingly charming and charismatic, but you'll later learn that there is more than what meets the eye. The narcissist to whom I'm referring to in this case, is a known assailant and his approach will be rather direct as he scouts for a potential "supply." His "type" is anyone whose value is beneficial to him.

Cue flashback. He was smooth, well dressed, handsome as hell and mannerly; he was every mother's dream. He had a smile that would soon be hard to forget; I remember because he had one abnormally deep dimple. I met him in church, he insisted on holding a door open for me. I was skeptical of him from the start. He felt oddly familiar, although it was the first time we had spoken; I knew I had met him before, but at that moment, I couldn't remember from where. He knew me too, and he also knew that eventually, I would stop trying to figure it out. As I walked through the door, which he held open, I conveniently walked into his trap. I may not have been his plan initially, but it turns out, I was his type. He somehow quickly recognized a potentially new supply and couldn't pass up the opportunity. Oh, be careful brown eyes what you see; for sometimes sticking to the plan is best.

Profiles are created, and details about the captive are collected and studied well in advance. In this story, it would appear that I'm the captive. I'm your average plain Jane; don't get me wrong I'm a looker, just probably not the girl you'd pick out of a crowd first. I'm a popular introvert, loyal, honest, passionate and assertive. I pride myself on being ambitious and incredibly self-sufficient. I came from a decent and loving home, went to a private school and later attended college, where I obtained a Bachelor's Degree in Nursing. I consider myself the ultimate package. It's a common misconception though, that abusers go for broken people. Rather, they tend to be attracted to someone's strengths as they enjoy the challenge. Highly successful, kind and sociable people commonly end up in relationships with them. I'm forgetting something... Oh yea, I'm extremely empathetic!

A toxic environment is any place or behavior that causes harm to an individual's overall well-being. This type of environment can be a detriment to both the empathetic person and the narcissistic person. An empathetic child in this setting will grow into a person who seeks love, approval and affection from others as an adult. Furthermore, they may become co-dependent and lack boundaries. A narcissistic child who grew up in a toxic home will grow to seek recognition and compliance from others as an adult. Their own emotional needs were never met, so they become emotionally irresponsible. Like the empathetic child, the narcissistic child is needy and likely struggles with co-dependency as they rely on others for their supply. The empathetic person accepts blame from themselves and others, while the narcissist projects blame onto others. Similarly, to the relationship of protons and electrons, the opposite charges are attracted to one another; there is no surprise that the narcissist is drawn to an empathetic person. The symbiotic relationship is of a parasitic one, the empathetic person gives, and the narcissist takes. The empathetic person has a need to fix; the narcissist has a void he wants to fill.

Chapter 3

THE HOSTAGE SITUATION

J an-Erik Olsson, a convicted felon, absconded while on a furlough from prison, in the year 1973. At the Norrmalmstorg square in Stockholm, Sweden, this fugitive casually waltzed into the Sveriges Kreditbank Bank undetected, with a concealed firearm. In an attempt to rob the bank, four hostages were taken captive.

The Norrmalmstorg Bank robbery was unlike any other seen in history. It made its debut as the first criminal event to be covered by live television in Sweden; and would soon capture the interest of each person watching around the world. What made the affair even more of a phenomenon was the unexplainable empathy that the captives developed for their captors during this six-day hostage crisis.

What really happened in the vault on that sunny day in 1973? You would think that being held up for six days would be the most gruesome experience, right? Well, according to the hostages, it was quite the opposite. Despite a witness report of a hostage being shot in the leg, the hostages and captors developed a rather relaxed relationship, including sexual relations. The captors and captives were on a first-name basis by day two; they shared stories and quickly forged a friendship of sorts.

Eventually, the hostages expressed more fear of the police than their captors, stating that the police's irrational actions would get them killed, rather than be of any benefit to them. These females famously formed an unusual bond with their captors and were purposeful about protecting them against the authorities. Olsson was later charged, convicted, and sentenced to ten years in prison. Despite forming a relationship under such dark circumstances, the hostages sympathized with their captors and refused to testify against them in court. These hostages developed such a strong bond with their captors that they even made routine jailhouse visits to them. When empathy and loyalty go wrong.

The puzzling actions of the hostages led to a great deal of scholarly interest in the case. One of the hostages, Elisabeth Oldgren, admitted to the psychiatrist that she was unsure why she felt the way she did, or why she didn't hate him. Oldgren further questioned if something

22

was wrong with her. The term known as Stockholm syndrome was coined in light of this particular situation; while it's not a formal diagnosis, it's a psychological concept used to explain responses such as a hostage becoming emotionally attached to or befriending their captor. This is definitely not your average love story. Not even Bonnie & Clyde's fiasco could measure up to this taboo encounter.

Stockholm syndrome was officially brought to international attention and it was used to explain several similar cases that occurred in history. In 1974, one year after the Norrmalmstorg Bank robbery, Patty Hearst, an American newspaper heiress, was kidnapped by the Symbionese Liberation Army. She eventually helped her captors rob a bank; she later pledged her allegiance to the group expressing support for their militant cause. Another example where a captive showed grave concern for their captor's wellbeing was in the case of 25 year old Mary McElroy. In 1933, Mary was abducted from her home and held for ransom for 29 hours; she was treated well during her captivity. Mary was rescued by the authorities, who later sent her captors to trial. Mary was so concerned for her captors that she even reached out to the Governor to request a reversal of her captors' harsh sentencing; when that was denied, Mary visited them in prison and maintained a friendship with them. Years later Mary committed suicide, leaving behind a note which stated, "My four kidnappers are probably the four people on earth who don't consider me an utter fool."

To be held against your will means that the circumstances have shifted out of your favor and control no longer belongs to you; desperation feeds your need for survival and 'by any means necessary' is the thought pattern developed. The victims will perform one out of two acts at this point. Gratitude and devotion to the captors may occur. The captors may utilize threats of harm towards their victims; this is done to establish fear. When no harm comes to the victims, the hostages feel as though they have been spared and perceive this as an act of kindness. On the other hand, the hostage discovers that to survive, they must become dependent on and compliant with their captors as these are traits that typically please these types of individuals. Mental health experts suggest that this is similarly seen as a protective strategy and coping method for victims of emotional and physical abuse.

At some point in our lives, we all become "hostages;" either it's our traumas that make us prisoners in our own mind and in turn, we become hostages to something rather than of something; we become hostages to our past. Perhaps it is the situations we find ourselves in, whether it was knowingly or unknowingly. The fact remains, it's still a hostage crisis, and somehow, we all ended up in the same place at the same time with a mutual feeling that we may not be able to escape. In summary, you never really leave a hostage crisis as the same person.

Chapter 4

THE NEGOTIATOR

N egotiations in a hostage crisis are typically based on the Behavioral Change Stairway Model, which includes active listening, displaying empathy, and establishing rapport. Additionally, obtaining a certain degree of trust can gain influence; this may or may not lead to a behavioral change, which is ultimately the goal. The ability to actually acquire the items being demanded limits what a negotiator can offer to the hostage-takers. Consultation with the situation commander and high-ranking political officials are necessary. The Swedish Attorney General allowed Olsson's former cellmate to be released from prison and join him at the bank during the infamous Norrmalmstorg robbery. He also requested a fast car, cash and weapons. In the beginning, demands are often unreasonable. The negotiator can progressively reduce the rigorousness of the captor's request by offering minor grants. The process of negotiating proves vital to achieving a peaceful resolution. Even if there is no intention of granting the demands, always let the enemy think they've won.

Let's see how it works: Miss J was a forensic psychologist brought in to work closely with the hostage negotiation team. It had been three days since the team had any sleep; some had not even seen their families. It was safe to say that everyone was exhausted. She looked up at the sun that glared profusely and intently even through her tinted ray ban lens; she held up one hand to her face to provide additional shade. For some reason, the sky looked notably different, and somehow, she knew that today would work in her favor. Her unspoken communication with the sky was interrupted by a distant pitter-patter; it was one of the officers on duty who shouted, "Hey, you're needed in the command center, we need you to take this call. He asked to speak specifically to you." "Okay, I'll be right in," she responded. She carefully maneuvered around the many drop cords and lines in the tent where she had been summoned. While accepting a cup of coffee given to her, she adjusted her headset and did what she does best, she negotiated.

"Hello, Miss J here. And what should I call you today?"

"Hello Miss J. I'm glad that you could take my call. King is fine."

"Wow, what a powerful name selection. Are you aware of the definition?"

"No, educate me."

"Firstly, it is a male ruler who inherits the position by right of birth. It can also describe the most important Chess piece. Do you play Chess or any games for that matter?"

"I'm good at a lot of things, and games would definitely be one of them, Miss J!"

"Good! In a game of Chess, each player has a king, which the opponent has to checkmate to win. The king can move in any direction. Listen carefully; what that means is we both need to be calculated in our moves and play correctly for the odds to work in both our favors. Do you agree?"

"I'm listening…"

"I believe I am in a position to help you King, and I'm sure you can help me as well. Let's talk some more. Care to tell me how you are feeling? Also, why did you choose to change your name today?"

"I feel like I'm on top of the world and no one can tear me down or make me feel bad today. I choose new names because I like the idea that I can be a different character every day." "So, I have a question King, you don't find it exciting just being yourself? Wouldn't that make it difficult for people to relate to you or understand what you need? Needs are important so tell me, what do you need today?"

"I want to go public. I've always wanted to be famous and I love to be the center of attention. I always say any publicity is good publicity."

"Okay, I will need 24 hours to make a few calls and the necessary arrangements, but first, I need proof, King. I need proof that everyone is alive and well. I will grant your request, but I will need two hostages to be released unharmed in front of a cameraman and reporter to air your message live."

"Hmm, that's a rather large request Miss J. Why should I agree to this?"

"Well, I think it's matched by me holding up my end of the bargain; you should do the same rightfully so. Besides, what would your fans think? I know you would want them to know that you're not a bad guy, right?"

"You drive a hard bargain but okay Miss J, okay."

The story continues, two things occurred as King slipped up big time! He got distracted and he temporarily forgot his goal. The live interview aired the captor and his identity as the perpetrator had now been discovered. Moreover, the cameraman and reporter who were allowed access were undercover police who engaged in immediate and aggressive measures to dismantle the hostage situation; snipers were also in place and ready to respond. Miss J breathed a sigh of relief as she removed her headset and watched the SWAT team perform a crisis entry on live television. In the end, not one hostage was physically harmed, and King was disarmed as he was removed from the building. Miss J couldn't help but notice the calm nature in which King left the building; he didn't resist at any point. She thought to herself, "The reason he didn't fight was because he knew he would be caught." She also caught sight of the unremorseful look on his face that day. She knew he would do it again!

As you can see, during a heist, plans can backfire; things can spiral out of control, then before you know it, the cavalry is brought in, and you're caught. Remember those previous lessons "...they were all caught, not because of a lack of preparation, but because they were either too eager, too fearful, or too distracted." King became cocky in his attempts and became messy with his plans. He got distracted and was too eager; when these two things occurred, the goal was forgotten and he was caught.

PART TWO

THE HEIST

"70 % of people who start a plan
quit! Not you...not this time..."

Chapter 5

THE CYCLE

A buse is a pattern that is established over time. It involves subtle to severe acts of violent behaviors towards an individual. These acts range from emotional abuse, manipulation and intimidation to any force used to cause physical pain or any kind of injury. Even controlling a person's income or withholding finances is considered abuse. In the case of narcissistic abuse, one of, or in most cases, all of these acts can be identified. Regardless of the type, all are performed with the sole intent to obtain control or maintain power over another person. There are several similarities between both the Abuse Cycle and the Narcissistic Cycle Models. In both instances, the partner primarily experiences the feeling of walking on eggshells, reconciliation, trials and finally, the calm before another storm.

Abuse isn't always easy to recognize; this is because oftentimes, there is dissociation observed from both sides of the spectrum. The first being, when the victim is no longer able to identify the treatment being experienced as abuse; psychological damage encountered over time creates a false sense of safety. The second is when a person outside of the relationship is unable to make a connection with abuse and the abuser. In this case, abuse is overlooked because the abuser has mastered the art of deception. In the public's eye, the abuser appears to be charming and helpful, which misrepresents the abuse. Abuse is often missed due to indirect manipulation, which can lead to the isolation of the partner, while the abuser maintains a favorable image to those outside of the relationship. This is a mind game commonly utilized by the narcissist. For example, during pillow talk with the partner, he may share false information about another person outside of the abuse, while simultaneously painting a negative picture about the partner to another outside of the relationship. This is likely to achieve the narcissist's goal of turning the partner and the other person against each other, ensuring that neither person approaches the other about the abuse taking place, thus effectively isolating the partner; as previously mentioned.

Once a narcissist enters your life, he will soon consume your entire being. The Idealize, Devalue, Discard and Hoover Cycle is the narcissist's go-to formula and the basis of domestic violence. It is a slowly dehumanizing and purposeful soul rape that takes place without anyone noticing, sometimes not even the victim. Simultaneously, the victim of abuse experiences The Five Stages of Grief & Loss: Denial, Anger, Bargaining, Depression, and Acceptance, which may not necessarily occur in this particular order. It is imperative that you understand the whirlwind. This may have been a heist initiated by the narcissist and intended to leave you as the victim; however, you will later see that you will become the leader of a heist of your own.

Chapter 6

DENIAL

T he Illusion Truth Effect is based on the idea that false information after repeated exposure can be perceived or accepted later as truth. A study in 1977 tested the theory that even if someone knew the correct answer to a question, they could be persuaded to believe otherwise through hearing an incorrect answer repeatedly, proving that what sounds familiar is truth rather than what is rational or logical. Just as this technique is used as a marketing strategy, the narcissist uses the same as an emotional manipulation technique. Aldous Huxley said it best "Facts do not cease to exist because they are ignored." Believing what we are told versus what we can actually see is the definition of living in denial.

The act of denial tends to compensate for the initial shock one experiences when receiving bad news. We downplay the enormous sense of hurt and pain that loss brings, while simultaneously trying to come to grips with what actually happened; in short, we refuse to accept the reality of it all. So your Prince Charming isn't really charming at all, shocker! Wait, was his name even really Prince? In the initial stage, we doubt what's actually in front of our faces. If it looks like a duck and sounds like a duck, then it must be a frog. I know this because I understand him so well; this is what he wants to be deep down.

Let me stop you at stage one if you're new here. When someone shows you their true colors, don't try to paint them over. He actually did more than show me; he told me who he was, and you guessed it, I didn't believe him. Blatant denial! He made me think that he needed me; that he needed me to show him love, you know, real love. I felt like his childhood, maybe past traumas, exes, the relationship with his mother and the fact that his father wasn't a part of his life all may have been the reason for his narcissistic behavior. I thought everything and everyone was responsible for making him the person that I came to know. The eye-opener came later when I discovered that he was the only person not being held accountable.

He is drawn to your beauty, your strength and your kind and selfless nature because of his own emptiness. He has mastered the art of being attentive, generous, and impressive at first. He will shower you with compliments on every small detail giving you such intense attention that it's hard to believe he isn't your soulmate. "Where have you been all my life?" Enchanting promises will be made and he will spend excessive amounts of time and money on you. The narcissist essentially will praise you and often exaggerates the characteristics of his new supply. To his friends and associates, I was "Doc," remember who we are dealing with; I'm actually a Registered Nurse. They want to look good, so they have to draw you equal or better. I later learned that this was his tell, like in a game of poker. If he exaggerated your profession or accomplishments, for example, then he had his eye on you or was involved with you. Now would be a good time to tell you to run, but you probably won't. So, I'll just say, "Nice to meet you, fellow supply." Sidebar: This is also a manipulation tool used to evoke jealousy in the other players he has rounded up. It seems like a lot is going on here, but don't worry, you'll be an expert soon; if you do your research, you will see that his truth is always highly inflated.

A moment of reflection: I said, "Hey babe, I need some stuff from the store." He replied, "You remember the code right" and handed me the card. This was the norm for us, I had access to his bank account, cell phone and cards, I dealt with large amounts of cash on his behalf, he introduced me to his family, he made me feel like he trusted me and I could trust him. We talked about EVERYTHING and I felt like he was finally opening up to me; he expressed things that I thought only I knew. I was sold on this dream. At this point, who wouldn't be thinking, "This is it." I was so comfortable and I thought we were good... or I was being set right the hell up to believe that we were. Later, I felt the after-effects of the truth bomb. I must admit that early on in the relationship, he mentioned that he was not ready for commitment because of a previous break up; that was his disclaimer, or "get out of jail free card" for the abuse that would later transpire. I completely missed that he was never actually emotionally available, nor was he prepared to become so. As the empathetic person I truly am, I thought I could change his mind over time. You've heard how people tend to avoid the elephant in the room; well, I sat on the elephant and had the nerve to ask if it was even in the room. Hello D-E-N-I-A-L, meet delusional, and when deranged gets involved; what an awful combination we've created. By now, you're beginning to understand this disaster story.

So, back to what I was saying, you'll be mesmerized and feel so adored, loved and blah blah blah that the red flags will be missed. And then...BAM here comes that hard fall from fairytale to reality! In a relationship with a narcissist, we never see a need to get out immediately. Instead, we make excuses and try to fashion another course of action in the name of 'making it work.' Meanwhile, things continue to worsen, and you find yourself overdoing and overworking until you're completely exhausted. Have you ever watched an old cartoon where the characters seem to be running past the same tree and car? Well, welcome to the hamster wheel, it's a ride that never stops on its own, so it's either we ride until we are sick to our stomach or we dizzily stumble off.

The narcissist begins his vicious cycle with idealization, in the form of love bombing; this is what initially draws us in. It's similar to a moth drawn to a flame or a flying insect to a light. There is a theory behind this. Some bugs, in search of food or nectar, are attracted to artificial light because the light bulbs contain the same UV light that flowers reflect. The same occurs with the theory of denial, you are on a search for whatever it is and it "appears" to be just that with the attentive or overly concerned narcissist. You're instantly drawn in and find it flattering that he remembers every detail about your life, when in actuality, you've been misled.

In this stage, one of the three things that the narcissist depends on most becomes clearly visible:

attention. This is the most excellent form of narcissistic supply and what charges them enough to move on to the discard phase with no qualms. They whisper sweet nothings in your ear, and by nothing, I mean nothing; because it takes nothing from them to tell you exactly what you want to hear. In turn, you shower the narcissist with compliments and adoration; you praise them for being godsent. They already have a grandiose and idealized sense of self, so to hear what they think of themselves out of the new supply's mouth is orgasmic. The more they superficially feed your desire, is the more profoundly you feed theirs.

This stage is two-fold because the victim isn't the only person in denial. In fact, true denial is the narcissist himself. I wonder if he ever stopped to evaluate himself. Does he realize that this isn't real and I'd find out eventually? Does he know his actions actually hurt people? This brings me to my next question. After doing so well with the mirror effect (role and blame-shifting, we will discuss this later); Does he even realize that he is the narcissist? The answer is no. That's right; he has a personality disorder; I somehow keep forgetting about that. So, even if you pointed it out, he couldn't see it, narcissists can't help themselves, or maybe they don't want to change their warped concept or perception of themselves or the world. They deny having an issue to begin with. Pseudologia Fantastica, also known as pathological lying, is compulsive and habitual lying that leads to self-deception. The epitome of denial is when you can not only ignore but somehow convince yourself that a lie is the truth and live with it.

In the end, it was all a dream. I had a college lecturer, known for his wit, who often said in his Politics class, "They have been pissing on us for so long and calling it rain." I was flabbergasted. Remember, I told you this was the guy who your mom would love? It's hard to accept that he wasn't that person, especially when it catches us off guard. Having been finessed for so long makes one automatically disregard any evidence of truth; but Sis, it really wasn't rain.

Chapter 7

ANGER

A nger is the most common reaction to loss; one is expected to feel upset about losing something or someone. However, if a person remains in this stage for too long, anger transforms from a short-lived or quick response to a permanent state. Anger is an appropriate response when unforeseen circumstances arise in our lives; however, it should be short-lived. Anger that is allowed to fester has the potential to grow into a constant feeling of resentment, a sense of being mistreated, or rage. Unresolved anger will eventually consume your mind and may also manifest itself physically by taking a toll on your body. Caution: Do not allow a bad five minutes to become a bad day.

Imagine preparing for work, you take a look at the clock and realize that you are late! Just as you are about to leave, you get the feeling that you are forgetting something, but you dash for the door anyway. You look down and notice that your keys are not in its usual spot. You have two options. Option 1: You accept the idea of your loss and you say to yourself, "Okay, I'm upset because I am already late and now I have to take additional time to backtrack my steps to locate my keys, this is unfortunate." Yet, you continued with your day and decided to make the most of it, despite having an unforeseen late start. Option 2: You reject the idea of your loss, which results in blame-shifting. "Just great, I'm now late because I can't find these stupid keys." You're probably going to continue to project this anger onto others in traffic, the person that allegedly stole your parking space, and the lady that 'deliberately' messed up your lunch order feeling like everyone is out to get you and life is unfair. In this instance, you blamed the loss of your keys for your tardiness, which created a permanent condition.

I initially experienced the stage of anger when I was no longer in denial. The truth finally hit me; the narcissist wasn't what he pretended to be, nor what I made myself to believe he was. The problem was, as Ovid put it, "Suppressed grief suffocates, it rages within the breast, and is forced to multiply its strength," and boy did it multiply. Hi, I'm Option 2! I mentioned earlier, in Chapter 5, that we all experience The Five Stage of Grief & Loss, and for some people, the order may not be the same. Well, let's just say honeyyy, I experienced this stage more than once! Honestly, I was angry for a long time and that general anger lingered straight through to the final stage of Acceptance. All of those intense emotions continued to brew until they became fury, and trust me; it can truly turn you into someone you don't even recognize. When the man behind the mask was completely exposed and the scales were removed from my eyes I became aware of my situation and my intuition, which always existed, kicked into gear and worked overtime. I was so, so done; I resented him, and every female he had relations with previously. But more so, I was angry with myself! I was, in fact, becoming bitter.

I told myself countless times that I wasn't going to say anything else to him, but then an "As a matter of fact, I think it's funny how..." moment would present itself. Okay, to be frank, I honestly texted him every time I thought of something new and got myself upset all over again. The texts pretty much went like this or any other thought that popped up in my mind at the time:

"I watched a movie the other day, and I remember a character that had an illness that couldn't be cured, funny how you're dying the same way. It's scary how people are alive, but their

soul is already dead, it's only a matter of time for you! You thrive off of being a joy stealer and sucker. You destroy people's lives because you don't have peace in your own. You want love so bad and the only way to get it is to pretend to be someone else. The sad thing is the mask comes off eventually and people soon see that the "show" is over."

"...You're not upset with me; your demons hate that I can see them. You always make reference to my eyes, now I know you weren't so captivated by them, but they became your obsession because you knew they could see the depths of your soul like no one else could..."

The partner that once made you feel so significant, the one that you thought put you on a pedestal, in fact, placed you back on the shelf. He got bored playing with you and like any valuable toy, you were simply added to a collection. The honeymoon stage may last weeks, months or even years, but ultimately cannot be continued because it genuinely never existed. The truth is, you will never see this man again because he was simply a fragment of both your imaginations.

On to the Devaluing stage. Something triggered or propelled the narcissist into this stage sooner than he expected. "Who likes getting caught," was his response after once again being confronted. When the narcissist feels threatened, their defense mechanism kicks in and narcissistic anger or rage is observed. When a partner can no longer be controlled through manipulation, the narcissist's fears and insecurities are heightened or vaguely recognized. Consequently, they respond violently and seek revenge. Be sure to note that there is no limit to what they would do to hurt you once you are placed on their naughty list. Long story short, I bruised his ego by calling him out – that's called Narcissistic injury. Injury, to them, is seen as deliberate and blatant disrespect, so things went downhill from here, and so did the respect.

In the movie Gaslight, made in 1944, a man manipulates his wife almost to the point of insanity. Gaslighting is a tactic employed to make one question their own reality, memory and perception. I had a similar gaslighting experience. It was quite frustrating when I was made to believe that I didn't see what I saw. It was even more aggravating when he tried to convince me that I misread and misunderstood provocative photos and suggestive text messages sent by 'friends.' According to him, I was always overreacting. Anything he didn't like or the simplest of conversations turned into arguments. The silent treatment was a regularly used punishment against me because of my perceived "constant rebellion." He would ghost me for quite some time and then returned like absolutely nothing happened, or if he needed a favor. This hot and cold game was frequently played.

Remember how I said, rejecting the idea of your loss results in blame-shifting? He is a pro at misconstruing interpretations and will somehow convince you that whatever happened is your fault. In the blink of an eye, he will turn those tables on you, just like a DJ. The narcissist reverses roles through projection. I know the feeling all too well; you're left deeply confused and questioning, "What the hell did I do wrong?" Simply put, he deflects everything on to you and suddenly, you become the issue or the problem; this is all a distraction. With you distracted, it's so much easier for the narcissist to shift blame and somehow end up becoming the victim rather than accept responsibility as the perpetrator.

Reactive abuse occurs when the abuser has exhausted the victim's tolerance, which elicits abusive behavior from the victim; essentially, the victim becomes fed up and lashes out in response. As a result of this response, the original victim is now accused of being the abusive person by the original abuser, but it was merely an act of defense to hold on to any self-respect that the victim had left. The narcissist will use this moment to capitalize on adding to his artillery by presenting this evidence to anyone willing to listen, to build the real victim's profile as the perpetrator/ abuser, while he appears to be the victim.

There was an image online with two characters being filmed during a chase. From a full view of this scene in the illustration one of the characters (The Narcissist) is chasing the other character (The Victim) with a knife. However the movie camera screen in this illustration only captures an image of the victim's shoulder, leg and pointed shoe (which resembles a knife) as he is running away; while the Narcissist's arm that is not wielding a weapon is captured in the same frame while he is chasing the victim. The cropped version as seen on the movie camera screen gives the appearance that the victim is the weapon wielding aggressor and the narcissist is the frightened victim. If you were able to see that image in your mind then you will have no problem understanding how the narcissist presents himself. That illustration depicts how the narcissist always presents a cropped or edited version of an event or story to others from the perspective that he is not the aggressor. For the victim this is always frustrating because the full version of the story, the truth, of what transpired is never told by the narcissist.

You will get to the point where anger subsides and eventually, you're over it. I promise it gets OLD! After you realize that the 'Mighty Morphin Power Ranger' act still fuels him, and ANY action or reaction at this point will suffice the narcissist. He knows it's only a matter of time before he loses you entirely; you're onto him.

Chapter 8

BARGAINING

I n Kubler-Ross's cycle of grief, the third stage is bargaining. In this stage, we seek ways to avoid having to experience what we deem the 'bad thing,' or, in this case, the inevitable thing. Bargaining is, in essence, an expression of optimism that the bad news is somehow reversible.

Have you ever been in a situation where you desperately needed God to intervene? Well, for me, it was the first time I received the news of my mother's diagnosis. I was crushed when I learned that she had developed colorectal cancer. How is that even possible? And Why her? I cried out to God, "...If you could just change the doctor's report, God, I promise to repair our relationship". My mom and I were not exactly in the best space seven years ago. I'm sure you can relate; yeah, you remember that stubborn, younger version of yourself, who always thought your parents were against you. Will Smith said it best in a song, "Parents just don't understand." Whatever it was then, I just knew I couldn't imagine living without her. "Please, God, don't take my mom away from me." I pleaded.

Desperation is the feeling that you have when you are in such a dire situation that you will try anything to change it. I'm a firm believer that with a little hard work and effort, anything could thrive. Even this relationship with a narcissist! As with any issue taking place in my life, I once again turned to God, whom I didn't consult about this 'entanglement' to begin with. So here I was on a three day fast asking Him to change this person so we could make sense. I later learned that God doesn't necessarily give us the answers that we want, but He gives us what we need to be at peace; this is what I needed to understand.

It's like when the fat lady gets ready to sing. You know it's coming, she is on the stage, the music is playing, but instead of listening to the beautiful and somewhat painful rendition, you close your eyes and shove your earpods into your ears. If you can't hear or see it, it's not really happening right? Spoiler alert the opera is about to conclude.

Speaking of singing, ever noticed how there is always a song for precisely what you're feeling.

"Surrender", written by Natalie Taylor and her husband, John Howard, is about the hardship experienced in a relationship and its eventual demise. The lyrics are as follows:

"We let the waters rise
We drifted to survive
I needed you to stay
But I let you drift away
My love where are you? My love where are you?

Whenever you're ready (Whenever you're ready)
Whenever you're ready (Whenever you're ready)
Can we, can we surrender
Can we, can we surrender
I surrender

No one will win this time
I just want you back
I'm running to your side
Flying my white flag, my white flag
My love where are you? My love where are you?

Whenever you're ready (Whenever you're ready)
Whenever you're ready (Whenever you're ready)
Can we, can we, surrender
Can we, can we, surrender

I surrender

Oh, I surrender"

Like a textbook example of a victim of abuse, I forgot why I should have been upset with him and ended up apologizing to try to win his forgiveness. Abuse amnesia is commonly observed when a person is still fixated on the success of an obviously failing relationship and is still hoping that their abuser would make a 180 degree turnaround for the relationship to succeed. "No one will win this time, I just want you back, I'm running to your side, Flying my white flag, My love where are you?" "...can we surrender" conveys the need to stop resisting and submit to the enemy or opponent right?

Bargaining is done to change an outcome for a more favorable one. It's normal to try to bargain when you find yourself in a hopeless situation. You begin to think about things you could have done better or even different to gain a more favorable outcome. We trick ourselves into hanging on to this relationship. We start to feel obsessed with trying to repair what was broken a long time ago. The more our efforts are ignored, the more persistent we become. Bargaining essentially allowed both of us to buy time, of course, for different reasons.

Mirroring is used to imitate another's actions in hopes of evoking empathy. Here you can expect them to make promises to change or suddenly start doing things you spoke about in the past. I fell for the narcissist's "Sorry, not sorry" apology and "You'll never find someone like me and I'll never find someone like you, so let's just make it work" line. We began to talk about a future together, even kids. He expressed that he wanted to do more together, take professional photos and vacation together. And like a true Strombus Gigas, I was in the middle of planning a full-on photoshoot and almost booked a cruise! Put me in the bag and beat me.

As we now know, the intentions of a narcissist are never pure and they always have an ulterior motive. While I had hoped to revive a relationship where rigor mortis had clearly set in, his idea of buying time was to simply switch up his manipulation techniques. This was done to prolong sucking my power to fuel his own. Yup, you're still valuable to him and he does not want to lose his supply. Your battery life just plummeted to 25%, by the way.

Chapter 9

DEPRESSION

N arcissists hate losing their supply, so the Devalue stage tends to last longer than any other. It begins subtly and continues covertly until the Discard stage. Whether or not this occurs is a well thought out and carefully calculated decision IN THEIR GAME of Chess. It depends on two factors: 1) How much battery life you have remaining; in the event, they can still get one last jump or charge from you. 2) How much of a threat you pose to expose them. They know deep down how much you've figured out and now realize that they have underestimated your wit. The Discard phase is the time where they are least in control of the situation, and although clever, they are unsure of your next move. Therefore, this will send them spiraling into paranoia, wondering who has spoken to who and who knows what.

It's personal now, so the narcissist will generally attack first. If you pose a threat to them, they'll become the most devious and dreadful being; it's inconceivable how ruthless they can actually become. If you haven't upset the fake routine, then you've probably steered clear of this side of him. Buckle up because the threats and scare tactics will definitely intensify. Smear campaigns are intended to discredit your account of events, all in an attempt to ensure the success of your mental demise. These campaigns are also meant to detach you, like removing the rotten apple to stop the whole bunch from spoiling. Know that before the end of this relationship, this serial abuser had already long planted a seed in the minds of the persons that you had hoped would side with you and believe me, he's undoubtedly offered a rather colorful and astonishingly credible sounding version of the truth. Remember the strategies of isolating the victim and filling his artillery with evidence against you that we spoke about earlier? In other words, save your energy, Sis. To the new target and followers, you're unstable and jealous. It's no wonder they never believe your warnings; they've been told that you were crazy! But what 'You're crazy' really meant was: I lied to you, I cheated on you, I gaslighted you, I abandoned you when you needed me, I made everything your fault, I twisted every argument, I broke down your self-esteem, and I was never accountable, and I never will be.

Trying to defend yourself against a narcissist's smear campaign is as useless as trying to remove water from a sinking boat while drilling a hole. Attempts to save your reputation, believe it or not, will make the situation worse. Flying Monkeys is the term given to the individuals that the narcissist uses as crutches. His fan club really can't see his wrongdoings. These are the loyal and reliable supplies, new supplies and his mother! It always gets worse before it gets better is what 'they' say. What 'they' neglected to tell you was how bad things would really get. You're distraught and rightfully so; he has managed to turn people against you almost effortlessly, yet you have done nothing wrong. You feel absolutely defeated and all alone. How is it that NO ONE else was able to see what you could see? Don't they have eyes?

Nobody: Post on WhatsApp.

Me: "Hey girl, I see you know…"

Her: "… Yes, I do. He is well known, respected and loved."

Me to myself: -Slaps face emoji. "You've got to be effing kidding me."

Despair is described as deep sadness or loss of hope. I lost hope in many things, particularly my dreams of a fairytale ending and my intuition. Now that I think about it, the hardest part wasn't losing him; it was coming to grips with the fact that I negotiated my respect. Additionally, I fell for his potential, having known better and having seen the warning signs as well as the patterns. What the heck was happening to me? His happiness had obviously trumped mine. The more I became aware of the fact that I needed to leave, the harder it became to get out of the quicksand. "You can't keep dancing with the devil and wonder why you're still in hell." I'm not sure who said this, but it's a big fact!

I looked directly at myself in the mirror and still couldn't recognize the image that looked back at me. I was beyond exhausted, and it showed; it took a toll on my mental and physical well-being. I was unable to sleep, unable to eat and with all that was happening in my life at that time, this was the straw that broke the camel's back. I had just returned to Nassau after serving in Abaco during hurricane Dorian. It was indeed a life-changing and traumatic encounter; surviving a narcissist is a similar feeling. Your life will never be the same. Even when you get out of the storm, in due time, the effects of post-traumatic stress disorder will eventually present itself. After months of not feeling like myself, avoiding people and not doing the things I loved, I remember finally getting out. I attended my godchild's birthday party. Her uncle, who happens to be a doctor, looked at me and said, "Jem, how have you been, like how have you really been?" The look of grave concern in his eyes was enough to convince me I needed to talk to someone.

This is the part nobody likes to talk about. I was not okay and hadn't been for a long time. I had been diagnosed with mild depression. In more detail, it was "emotional stress that occurred as a result of injury or severe psychological shock." I was hurt and I needed help. The truth is, this whole ordeal had a greater impact on me than I realized. This chapter was the most difficult one for me to write. I knew what it felt like to be at an all-time low, and the thought of revisiting this stage, even for the sake of writing this book, was extremely difficult.

I discovered a stage not usually identified when grief or loss is discussed, but I think it happened somewhere in the middle of depression and acceptance, the healing phase. It was either I faced the music or lose myself completely. I've been in enough situations to know that you have three choices, you either sink, swim or become the captain. I genuinely believe that every single person has to go through something that destroys them so they can figure out a few things. In reconnecting with God, I rediscovered myself! I delved deeper into His word, and I learned that I had to forgive my abuser as well as myself to completely heal. In summary, this entire ordeal was a blessing in disguise. Trust me, keep reading, you will thank me later.

To discard is to get rid of something. It is further defined as getting rid of something or someone that is no longer useful or desirable. I was no longer useful and no longer a conquest. He was no longer desirable, and I began to accept that I couldn't fill the emptiness he was continually seeking to fill.

Chapter 10

ACCEPTANCE

A cceptance means that you have chosen to make an effort to understand what is now the 'new reality,' and you now recognize that it can't be changed. This doesn't mean that you will automatically be okay or that the sadness would suddenly disappear. Acceptance doesn't mean that you don't think about the loss; neither does it mean that you somehow forget everything you have gone through. The best way to cope is to allow yourself to feel. There is no specific period of time for you to complete this process. I don't want you to think that you have to ignore anything, what happened to you is real, and it did and probably still does hurt. Give yourself credit, though; the fact that you are now able to identify what has happened and you are able to process the loss, without denial, proves that you are in a better place.

Take a look at this scenario: Rider and his Dad were on a road trip; they entered a tunnel which was long and dark. The only thing that could be heard was the echo from the car's engine. Rider was afraid of small enclosed spaces, so his dad intentionally drove through these tunnels from time to time to show him that he would always come out okay. What seemed like hours to the anxious child had been less than ten minutes. He closed his eyes really tight, and suddenly his dad said... "We're almost to the end, son, you can go ahead and open your eyes. I can see the light at the end of the tunnel," the son sighed heavily in relief. The moral of the story is life will sometimes take you through what may seem like a dark situation, but trust that you are never alone and no matter how long it may seem, God will always provide a way of escape! I read a post on a social media platform that said, "Don't let anyone tell you that your love is determined by the level of pain you can endure. Loving someone means holding them accountable, even if that means you have to let go." The day finally came when my head and heart agreed on what needed to be acknowledged and accepted.

You're scrolling on social media and you see a video, cue music. This is the moment every girl dreads after a break-up. We are generally okay until we see them with someone else. He and his 'new friend' look happy. He is having fun and doing the things you've always wanted, but with someone else. I get it; it feels like a blow to the stomach, right? Please let me help you with that feeling. If you've been following, you know by now that you have dodged a bullet, sister. Newsflash, that man hasn't changed. In fact, he hoped it got to you. That video did exactly what it was intended to do; to make you regret the break-up. This is called the Hoover technique; it is utilized as a means to suck their supply back in. If that did not work, be prepared for random photos to be shared in hopes of evoking emotions from memories and random texts reminding you of things you did together or places you went together. He may even pretend to be down or depressed about a situation and insist on your help or advice to make you worry or show concern. At this point, we have already seen this culprit in action and have accepted, just as my dad often told us growing up, that a leopard doesn't just wake up one day and change his spots. A narcissist can't change who he is either.

The attention seeker will do virtually anything for the sake of attention. The key to responding to these hoovering tactics is not to respond to him. Disconnecting and disengaging from him limits interaction and eventually starves the narcissist. The 'reluctant acceptance' is an inevitable crisis that this aging narcissist will soon face. When the curtains close and the audience leaves, he will be alone and have to face himself. He has always known that his scam won't work so well when you are no longer young and naive. It certainly doesn't work as well when the only thing you have to show for your life is the same tired story you've been telling for years. Over time, the real person eventually is exposed and the cycle begins and then ends again, but more people will now discover who he truly is. The fan club, too, soon grows tired and they are not as willing to buy into his stories of blame and conspiracy. It's just not cute anymore; well, it never was. It's especially not cute when someone is old enough to know better and do better by now.

Do you remember growing up and hearing stories of the boogie man? Well, let me tell you another horror story. Narcissus was a Greek mythological figure and hunter known for his striking beauty. He enjoyed everything beautiful and was a proud man. He disdained those who loved him, even causing some to take their own lives to prove their devotion to him. Narcissus was so in love with his reflection that one day while admiring himself in a pool of water, he became so enchanted he was drawn in and he drowned. After any ghost or monster movie or story, I would be too terrified to turn my light off or even look under my bed to see if there was a real monster. Manipulation is kind of like the boogie man; it scares you enough to discourage you from discovering the truth. But when you get older, the stories just don't scare you as much, and you finally realize that monsters are not real, just as in the case of the narcissist. Breaking free of the matrix is like being the sober individual at a party full of drunk people. My acceptance and the narcissist's 'reluctant acceptance' of this truth is what led to the end of his heist and the beginning of mine. This is how I became the mastermind of the greatest heist known to man and created a blueprint of my own to share with you.

PART THREE

THE TRIAL

"...Your Honor, thank you for your permission to approach the bench..."

Chapter 11

LIFE AFTER THE HEIST

Despite all that I have been through, I still do love fairy tales. I was 'shook' when a friend pointed out that we never really see the end after the 'happily ever after' of a Disney movie. The movie is now over, the tv is turned off and we go back to our normal lives. Have you ever thought about what life is like after the 'happily ever after?'

The end of a narcissistic relationship is similar to that of shattering glass. No matter how much you attempt to clean up the mess, you still find pieces later. Glass travels far, obviously. The mess this individual leaves behind travels even further; the impact lingers much longer than anticipated. So are the effects experienced after abuse.

In some instances, a narcissist's partner will experience general sadness and depression that could lead to suicidal thoughts or attempts. Others may develop a condition known as post-traumatic stress disorder (PTSD); this can occur after any traumatic event. People who have difficulty coping and adjusting often have triggers that can cause severe anxiety and uncontrollable thoughts about the event; they are likely to experience crippling fear, flashbacks or even nightmares. Symptoms can get worse and last for months, sometimes years, and eventually interfere with normal daily functioning. The symptoms of complex PTSD include the continuation of the cycle of abuse. Some people feel guilt and may be conditioned to think that this is what they deserve and the only type of relationship they will experience.

We move away from textbook explanations when we begin to highlight personal encounters. I have had the opportunity to speak directly with other women who fell in love with a narcissist and to hear second-hand stories about survivors of a mutual abuser. These were the stories of real women who encountered trust issues in relationships long after their abusive relationship ended. As a means of coping, protecting themselves and seeking comfort, some women turned towards romantic same-sex relationships or substance abuse in the form of drugs and alcohol. While others experienced general changes in behavior as a direct result of low self-esteem. These behaviors may have included becoming guarded, withdrawing or engaging in promiscuous behavior to fill a void, to feel wanted or to be loved. As for me, as mentioned previously, I didn't get much sleep and lost interest in a lot of things that I previously enjoyed. I had recurrent dreams, but one, in particular, stood out. I was trying to help a friend escape an abusive relationship. I helped her out of the house and she escaped, but the person in the dream began chasing me. I was literally on the run and no matter where I went, he found me. I soon realized it was a message for me. I needed saving, not my friend!

Please know that the abusive event is considered traumatic to the person experiencing it, not to an outsider or the abuser in the case. If someone says that you hurt them, you do not get to decide that you didn't. Read that again! There is no 'one size fits all' way to handle the issue of domestic violence. It is indeed a delicate one and should be dealt with on an individual basis and with professional and family support.

Chapter 12

KEY WITNESSES & CROSS EXAMINATION

Being the over-thinker that I am, I could not wrap my head around it. I still wanted to know why? What turned him into this monster? What hurt him? I thought back to the female that he allegedly placed on a pedestal, does she have a story too? I got in contact with her, and I could not rest until we spoke. This wasn't a 'coming to you as a woman call,' so I had no idea what I would say. Besides, he and I had already broken up, and this woman had moved on with her life years ago. I thought to myself, what if I triggered something by asking her to reopen this wound? Was it healed? Would she even be willing to talk?

"Hi, you don't know me, but I've heard about you, and we have someone who mutually connects us… Maybe you can help me to understand something a bit better." My mouth was dry and there was a huge lump in my throat as I spoke these words. I paid keen attention to her voice and the way she reacted when his name was called. Then came that sigh, instantly, I knew where this conversation would go as we connected without words in that brief moment. That was a familiar sigh. It was evident that his name had not been mentioned and was avoided for years, with good reason. I remember the way she told her story of her escape; it was planned well in advance. She rehearsed it over and over because she knew she couldn't afford to mess it up. She asked to meet him at a public place, and then she broke up with him. I felt like she did when we broke up for the 5th time, or maybe it was the 10th time that was serious. She confessed to me that when she broke up with him, she felt like such a heavy burden had been lifted off of her; when she shared this, I felt like my burden was being lifted too. She ran and ran and never stopped running! She said that it was the best feeling she had ever experienced. Suddenly, I didn't feel heavy anymore. There were no other questions to ask. I knew what I had to do now.

Three years, three hours and twenty-four minutes later, it all made sense. For once, I did not feel 'crazy'. For the first time in what seemed like years, I felt like someone finally understood! I would never forget that call because it was a day that she and I needed. She had not addressed issues that haunted her for years, which still affected her, and I needed help making sense of it all. I could not stop thinking about our conversation and I woke up the following morning in a manic state! I got angry, then I was filled with deep sadness as my heart was heavy, but then I got angry again. I paced my apartment and felt emotions that I had never felt before. After listening to her story, it was the first time that my sole focus was not on myself; I simply knew that I would be okay. I grew concerned about the other women I did not have an opportunity to speak with at that time; I was riled up on their behalf. They were the ones who had already developed trauma bonds and may have been experiencing Stockholm Syndrome. My heart went out to every female ever involved with him, even the new victims who had no idea what was coming. I thought about him doing that stupid wink or smirk at them, and then I exploded. This was the release I was waiting on for years!

Your Honor, thank you for your permission to approach and question the narcissist.

"You have to be a really messed up person to destroy your life and the lives of others. The biggest coward is a man who awakens a woman's love, with no intention of loving her. How do you live with yourself, or even sleep at night knowing the countless number of females you've affected? Some in deeper ways than you realize or even care to know. I'm talking physically,

emotionally, and psychologically. Between trauma bonds, Stockholm syndrome and PTSD, you've rounded up yourself a whole list of heinous crimes. You've scarred these women to the point of even turning to the same gender for love. You have no regard for your actions or human life, for that matter. You are the scum of the earth; at this point, dirt is better than you. Tell me: Do you have a heart or even a conscience?? I'm not even speaking for me because I'm not the only one you've come in contact with. I felt compelled to stand up to you for every female's feelings you've disregarded. Thank God I was one of the strong and lucky ones. You understand very little about how fragile the mind is!"

"Your judgment should be you on a court stand surrounded by the females you've used, manipulated, taken advantage of, lied to and essentially destroyed while 'having fun.' You need to know that your reckless pursuits have caused permanent damage. They should make you listen to each woman and look in every face while they give their accounts... You must know your actions come with consequences and your day is coming; the more souls you collect, the heavier your burden will be. I speak for every woman you've mishandled when I say you're sick, narcissistic, egotistical, pompous, and arrogant and you have no remorse. You prey on, study, stalk and play mind games with these women. You're pathetic! No additional charges have been made by others because some are too scared to make a formal *complaint, or some have run so far away from you; to ask them even to recollect those awful memories, would be asking them to relive that torture. And I just couldn't do that. Imagine the paranoia, anxiety and trust issues you either gave birth to or heightened. I'm no judge but, I sentence you to a lifetime of imprisonment. May you rot in your deeds. You're not worth my hate, even that's too good for you.*

Your Honor, these are my final words to the narcissist.

It felt so good to call my abuser out on his foul behavior. The first person that came to mind, as you may have guessed, was the stranger, who eventually became a friend, even though it was not what we expected. I Immediately contacted her to share my exciting news, and this was her response:

"Oh, wow, Jem! This really brought tears to my eyes because I felt every word you said to him and I, Rhondi Forbes, appreciate it. I thought about our conversation almost all day, but didn't want to keep messaging you and I even cried because that's a feeling I will NEVER forget and I don't wish that on my worst enemy. It's so crazy how another human being could be so destructive not only to others, but also himself and I pray he gets it together soon. I appreciated our talk last night and although I don't know you fully, I appreciate you. Not looking for a friend, but I am happy that I know another strong woman, someone who

has a head on her body, beautiful on the inside and out, and can stand up for other females who don't even have the words to say to him. It's a shame, but we'll overcome it hun. YOU WILL overcome this and look back at it and laugh."

This was a big changing moment for me; I felt a sense of justice. The narcissist thrives on targeting lone individuals. The response above, in particular, made me think. What if we, as women, stood by one another and formed allies? That day, I was able to see the bigger picture. There is definitely power in numbers, and fostering these types of relationships amongst survivors could perpetuate confronting abusers and rid them of their 'power.'

Surviving a narcissist is the most significant accomplishment any woman could achieve, and you ought to pat yourself on the back if you have survived. Go ahead, do it now! You are a survivor if you got to the end of the heist and escaped. You certainly are a survivor if you remain in your situation, solely because of circumstances, such as having kids involved or because you took a vow and are married. The fact that you have confronted your abuser, or now identified that patterns you have experienced are abusive; means you have already chosen a way out! Know that nothing that happened to you was your fault, you are still in control of your life and you control the ending of your story. I'm confident in your ability now to plot a heist of your own if the need ever arises again.

Chapter 13

VICTIM IMPACT STATEMENT

W hen I look at everything that I have endured, I wouldn't change a thing; in fact, I would have learned these lessons a little earlier, so I could help each one of you sooner. It would be so much easier to assume the role of victim; I mean, according to the definition, I was harmed and injured as a result of an event or action. But, that would not prove useful for me and certainly would not have inspired you. Today, I choose not to be identified as a 'sufferer,' which is a synonym for a victim, but rather, I'll coin my own term, a 'resilient bad a**.' Maya Angelo said it best, "I can be changed by what happens to me. But I refuse to be reduced by it." Life doesn't get easier, nor does it become more forgiving. We may overcome one battle while simultaneously fighting another, but that is what makes you stronger and more resilient.

I'm an empathetic person, that is who and what I am, and I don't apologize for it. I do not feel like I made myself a target because I am capable of showing great empathy. There are some advantages to being this type of individual. I can smell a lie from a mile away, I feed off of energy and if something is off, my antenna is activated instantly. I am more aware of my feelings and also conscious of the feelings of others. I am also very creative. While it is in my nature to empathize with people, I realized that in order to protect my energy, I have to: 1) Know what to deal with versus what to leave, rather than take on. 2) Know that there ARE people out there that WILL target you and TRY to take advantage.

Let me reiterate, being in a relationship with a narcissist has robbed you (also me); and the longer you stay, the more violently, pieces will be taken away from you without your permission. I don't know how far you are in your escape plan. There are some of you reading this right now that have never encountered a narcissist, but you are feeling a desperate need to try and salvage a relationship that you know is abusive, toxic or one that will inevitably lead to hurt and self-destruction. While others may wonder why is it so hard to let go of and move on from the loss of a previous relationship. I do believe that you cannot heal in an environment that hurts you.

Although the dynamics of my situation may be different from yours, one thing we may have in common is, we tried to blame ourselves for being a victim of a narcissist at one point or another. The truth is, you are not responsible! I repeat, you are not responsible for the way someone else treated you. There is no way you can be held accountable for somebody else's actions or traumas projected onto you. You are essentially responsible for your OWN emotions and responses.

Now that you've survived the narcissist, what's next? As stated earlier, I'm a strong believer that hurt people don't have to hurt people. There was a time when I felt that if I got him to feel exactly how he made me feel, then the hurt would disappear, but it didn't and my bitterness grew. Keeping the cycle going creates a domino effect and before you know it, there will be a lot of angry and 'hurt bombs' walking around. Let's stop the cycle if you haven't done so already. Begin by identifying and addressing your struggles and your past traumas so that you don't, in turn, project those unresolved issues or feelings onto another as it was done to you. I want you to know that this healing process is ongoing and sometimes feels longer than the actual encounter. There is no specific timeframe for it and there will be episodes of relapse. I'd be lying if I said that I was completely healed, and it would be ridiculous to believe that at the end of this book, you would be too. If you don't remember anything else I've said, please remember that you are now your top priority! You have spent years, some more than others, pouring from that same tainted, empty cup; let's polish you up and fill that glass. I prefer wine, but if you want to use water as your metaphor, that works too. Know that you have gotten back what rightfully belongs to you, so take this time to carefully pour back into yourself and celebrate the success of this heist.

This is certainly an experience that I would never forget. Although bent, sometimes beyond recognition, I was never broken! I learned some very valuable lessons, three of which stood out the most:

1) There are times that we must accept that people are exactly what we hoped they wouldn't be.

2) Potential will always remain potential.

3) The biggest lesson; allow no one to validate you. What begins will eventually end, so don't exaggerate people's presence in your life. What was meant to be a lesson or in your life for a season, we sometimes hold on to for longer than was intended. Nothing that is for you will ever miss you! So, no need to hold on so tight.

The narcissist I encountered has changed my concept of a partnership in a significant way. When I felt lonely, he pushed me back into the arms of God. He also pushed me closer to new and now meaningful people. Unbeknownst to him, his actions propelled me to strengthen existing relationships with friends and family. Always keep in mind that even though you are done with him, ten years later, he'll check back just to make sure that your verdict hasn't changed. Do not grant access to your life to people who have already messed up. His chances have expired, and besides, you've grown. Who he is looking for no longer lives there, and you've worked too damn hard to get your power back, so DO NOT go back.

Chapter 14

WITNESS PROTECTION

N arcissist: *Sits quite confused at the opposite table*... Awkward silence.

Me: Sips coffee slowly, "Yes, can I help you?"

Narcissist: "I'm sorry. I didn't mean to stare. I couldn't help but notice you were alone. And besides, you're very attractive."

Me: "Thank you for the compliment, and at the moment, yes, I am alone. You appear to be as well."

Narcissist: * Chuckles* "I enjoy being alone. But you look so familiar; I can't help but feel like we've met before..."

Me: "Oh, I don't believe we have. You see, I just moved recently."

Narcissist: "Oh, really, maybe I could show you around sometime." *Smirks then winks*

Me: *Packs items while standing* "That sounds great. Let me write down my address, 2989 Sycamore Street...."

Relax, don't panic! I'm not saying you have to live out the rest of your days in a witness protection program or anything, but at this stage, I think it's safe to say that you have learned a thing or two from him. He taught you that the best way to hide anything was to hide it in the open! Brilliant. Sometimes you have to pull a "him" on him to understand. He will search for you only to find that you no longer exist.

Narcissistic abuse is an opportunity to create a new you! What better time than now? It's all a part of the healing process; shed to grow! The process of ecdysis is also known as skin shedding. Snakes shed their skin to allow further growth and get rid of parasites attached to their old skin. He will wonder if it's you and then second guess his thoughts because you look so different yet so familiar. Leave him with the 'stretched skin' of the former you; he likes trophies, remember? At least, now he would have something to add to his collection because this will be the only trace of you that is left and the closest he'll ever be able to get to you again. By the time the narcissist realizes what's happened, you will be long gone. Back to the drawing board. You have a damn good prototype, just fix the glitches or the bugs, remove the damaged and unwanted parts and salvage the semi-functioning ones. And there you have it, a new version, you 2.0; healthy, conscious, and awakened with boundaries.

Chapter 15

CLOSING STATEMENT

As a little girl, growing up watching my parents really kept my fairytale hope alive. I always dreamed about a prince finding me, sweeping me off my feet and living in a palace happily ever after. Here I am now, 30 years old, and my princess gown no longer fits! Reality and life have added weight, reshaped me and convinced me otherwise. It has also brought a lot into perspective; therefore, I no longer love hard, I love accordingly.

They say you have three real loves in your lifetime and they all teach a specific lesson: your First Love, Painful Love and the Unexpected Love. Your first love sets the tone for all your other relationships. Let's stop there! I was following, until this part. This makes absolutely no sense! You're still reading my story, right? Because I'm pretty sure I did not write anything about riding into the sunset with this dude that is either no longer alive, lost or has gotten distracted along the way. They also say that your first love is the love you will never forget, and they will leave an imprint on your heart that will last a lifetime. Now, this part is true; my recollection of my first love was my fondest memory. I didn't have to think about it; it just happened.

People talk a lot about love. I thought I knew all there was to know about it, but it turns out I knew nothing. It took me so long to realize that my first love was actually the man that changed my diapers and sucked the snot out of my nose. My first love taught me how to ride a bike (failed attempt) and how to service a car (I don't think I recall all the lessons), but my point is, my first love was the first man I laid eyes on when I entered this world. Let's look at this statement again, "Your first love sets the tone for your other relationships." Now that I think of it, it does hold some truth! He is a wise love and has been preparing me from birth; lesson learned. He showed me what it first looked like to love someone and set the bar pretty high, but it was up to me to never drop that standard.

I remember one of the last conversations between the infamous narcissist and me. A few of his comments stood out to me:

"You have s*** mixed up... I'm not supposed to come into your life and make you happy..."

"...I'm not innocent in all of this, but it's about time that somebody gave you a reality mother f****** check."

" ...I'm not attacking you. I'm just saying don't throw stones when you have a glasshouse."

Although his thinking is usually self-centered and his perception is warped, he had a point this time (rolls eyes), and I admit he got my a** together and not just in terms of a clap back. What he intended to be negative was just what I needed to get my act together.

Welcome to the second type of love; Painful Love. Pain is intended to teach you a lesson you did not think you needed to learn. I thank God for saving me from what I thought I wanted. Here I was crying over these painful relationships that made absolutely no sense, nor did they have the ability to work. I didn't realize their only purpose was to expose my unhealed parts. The same experiences kept recurring, but the only difference each time was the person who held my interest. The reason I ended up staying in this phase for so long was because I missed the entire point, then some more of the point and then guess again, THE POINT. I tried to fix other people as a distraction to avoid fixing myself. Lesson learned: You attract what you need to heal, which leads you to find your final love. The Unexpected Love.

The third type of love we experience in life is surprisingly said to be the easiest love; the Unexpected Love. It teaches us how to feel love and give love correctly. The Unexpected Love is the love we never see coming. Daddy taught me what I should expect; then I learned what I did not want while simultaneously learning what I needed to fix, which was the last piece of the puzzle. In Chapter 10, I mentioned that we don't get to see what happens after the 'happily ever after' at the end of a fairy tale. Well, just like this particular love is unexpected, so is the end of this story. As the author, this ending is up to me, and I will give you the truth after the 'happily ever after.' Most people who have read this book thus far probably thought that this ending would have been Prince Charming finally making his late, but grand entrance. The biggest surprise or lesson is that this Princess saves herself! I was the love I needed and searched for all along.

Okay, so I see where I left you guys hanging. You probably wanted the ending that you see in those Lifetime movies, right? You know the ones where they say where the characters ended up or currently are in life! So let's recap, shall we? Here's 'the how it started versus how it ended' bit you're requesting.

Once upon a time in a land far away lived a beautiful, brave and fearless Princess. She later met an equally handsome and seemingly charming man, whom she thought was a Prince from a neighboring land. Time revealed that the so-called prince did not come from a royal background at all. Actually, his name was King, but he had no lineage to a royal family! You see, the fake prince knew that if he manipulated the princess to marry him, he would then become King, well, an actual King and rule the castle. Of course, he did his research well in advance. He knew that the princess was the next heir for immediate and automatic succession.

When the princess discovered King's secret, he grew angry and 'placed' her in a secret tower. Days turned to weeks, then years, and the princess was repeatedly tortured. Some days she got really sad, even despondent, and did not feel like a princess at all. One day she got so fed up and thought about an escape plan. As she paced around the tower, gathering her thoughts and rehearsing her plan, she heard noises in the distance. She soon discovered there was a chamber with other princesses. She was astonished when she learned how long they'd been there and that the reason for their incarceration was that they too found out that King wasn't a real prince. She quickly shared her escape plan and got all the other princesses on board.

The prince believed that to hide anything, it would be best to hide in the open, and there laid the key to the chambers! After freeing the other princesses, she promised each of them that she would help them to safety and that they would all leave alive. The time came where the princess and prince wrestled until dawn, and alas, he accepted defeat. He was then shackled and bound in his own chamber! As the princess got to the castle doors, to her discovery, the doors were never locked! They all escaped and never looked back.

How it ended... Cue, character profile narration, likely seen at the end of a movie:

"King, aka the narcissist, served a life-time sentence in his own prison. He literally rotted in his own deeds."

"The princess, now Queen, started an academy of her own where she taught other women how to become Queens and rightful successors of their kingdoms. She also threw in self-defense classes here and there (LOL). You never know when you'll need it."

Well, would you look at that? The Queen did, in fact, live happily ever after. Remember that thing about perspective? Well turns out it's also only part of a whole story. Stay tuned...

THE NARCISSIST'S CONFESSION

Dear Survivor,

You did not deserve the things I said and did to you, but I am not sorry for this behavior. I do understand, but I simply cannot relate to your pain. From a logical standpoint, I have processed that it is wrong; yet, my personality disorder makes me unable to sympathize with you or be remorseful. Sometimes I wish I could, but I cannot. You understand this, right?

As a child, I did not have many positive role models in my life and I never learned how to become a good person. I was never really shown love. People raised on love see the world differently from those who were raised on survival. I never shared this with you, but just like you, I could not understand why I was not loved. I was also hurt, betrayed, and abused. I hated feeling vulnerable and being sensitive because I was never taught to handle such strong emotions. Instead, I chose to believe that these were all characteristics of a weak person.

It was not easy getting this far in life, never being held responsible for my actions. So far, my narcissistic behavior has generally gone unnoticed because I know how to get others to trust me. It is this mask that I wear to hide my true colors. I also get by, by acting like a nice person; it is exhausting, but I have become comfortable with the idea. I have lied habitually for so long that I now believe my own lies. Do not you fall for my lies though! Even though I really want you too.

I targeted the wrong person this time; you have become aware that this mask I always wear is not real. I always knew you were too smart and you were right about me this entire time. It does not matter, though, I will become defensive, and I will attempt to destroy you or simply discard you. I deny the truth about myself. I am actually paranoid. I act confident, but I am shallow and insecure. The truth is, I act like I love myself, but I really do not. You should not wait for me to change because I most likely never will. I am incapable of love and no matter the amount of love and attention you give to me, it will never be reciprocated.

Every man tells a story about his past relationship and how his ex is a toxic crazy b****; just know that the ex is me! I am the toxic crazy b****. You never were. I will eventually destroy you and I intended to do so, believe me. If you care about yourself, you should leave. You can leave, even though I will manipulate you into believing that you cannot. I have no power. You are actually stronger than I am, but I will never admit this to you.

Sincerely,

The Narcissist

A LETTER OF APOLOGY & INTENT

Hey you,

I'm sure you don't even recognize me anymore; I've been absent and out of your life for a long time now. Know that this was the hardest thing I've ever had to do, but this is something I must confess. I wrote this letter to make things more transparent for you and to make peace with you. I knew that you'd read this letter when the time was right.

Let me begin by saying, I'm sorry, Jemeica P. Freckleton, if I ever made you feel like I never loved you. I really did, but I should have said it more. Instead, I let you believe that you were hard to love, that you had to find it elsewhere and that's where all your problems began. I broke you and because of that, you began to gravitate towards people who were also broken. You thought that if you nursed or nurtured them back to wholeness, then they would love you more, but they didn't. This ended in you developing a 'type,' and a wrong type at that. You weren't even aware of the cycle that you began. The more you gave, you received nothing in return.

Those unreciprocated or one-sided relationships made you feel like something was wrong with you. I didn't stand up for you and I didn't tell you that it was a lie. Let me say now, nothing is wrong with you, nor has there ever been anything wrong with you. You were convinced, though, and you blamed yourself. As a result of this, things continued to go downhill from there; you weren't happy with yourself, and nobody knew. I did, though, but I watched as your self-esteem and confidence dwindled almost to nothing. You continually found faults with your appearance, and this false insecurity pacified your need to know the real reason why your relationships failed.

Please don't hate me, I was supposed to be your friend, but I hurt you more than anyone else in your life. I've damaged you and sometimes I felt like it was beyond repair. I wanted to tell you, believe me, but things got so far out of control. How could I now admit that the reason no one could see how great you are is because I didn't make you aware? Instead, I made you toxic; I made you desperate, I made you hate being alone and I made you codependent. You rely on people a lot more than I remember you doing. Please let me help you with that. Think back to the time when you were braver. It was when you were a child and nothing phased you. For so long, you surely didn't need validation from anyone, and definitely not a man. Please try to remember this, it's important. I need you to do that.

I can't undo the things that I have allowed to happen to you, hell I wish I could put you in a time machine to take you back to a time before things got so complicated, but I can't. Enough of the excuses, truth is, I should have been there for you! You were lost and you looked everywhere for me, but I was nowhere to be found. That must have been really hard for you. I'm sorry.

I want to make it up to you. I want to be accountable now; I want to accept that it's partially my fault. I want to start over; I want you to start trusting me again. I never led you wrong, remember? You used to listen to everything I said. I want you to forgive me. I don't want you to continue to carry this burden any longer. You've been through so much! It's time to forgive yourself. I want you to know that I value you and that you are more than enough! You are strong, you are resilient, and I promise to never leave your side again.

Sincerely,

Me – your accomplice to our greatest heist ever

HELP RESOURCES

Remember that your wounds are not your fault; however, your healing is your responsibility. Be patient and gentle with yourself, Queen; you're doing well. Healing is a process and something we don't have to go through alone. In preparing a plan to move forward, remember that reaching out to your local church, family or friends you trust and getting the necessary professional help is vital.

Visit **www.fempowerment242.com** and subscribe for updates, news and information on domestic violence and narcissistic abuse through our weekly Podcast and blog. Please don't suffer in silence. Become a part of the movement today; we want to welcome you into our family through the Organization's Gal Pal Initiative.

FEmpowerment's vision is to provide the right environment with the proper support and helpful tools. Our team approach will effectively develop your innate abilities to transform you into a Strong, Resilient, Woke, and Empowered Woman. FEmpowerment's mission is to become a voice for the voiceless and a platform for all women. We are committed to raising awareness of the normalization of abuse. We speak not to be heard but rather speak up for what is right!

Other Professional Resources Include:

Local Counselors:

Harrison Thompson:

Relationship consultant, therapist, life coach, motivator, and vlogger

You can book appointments and make inquiries through the office at: **1 (242) 356-7983 or 4. Or via Email:** http://www.harrisonhelps.com/contact.html

Dr. David Allen:

Private practice in Psychiatry and individual therapy. Sandyport Beaches Resort in Nassau, Bahamas.

For more information, he may be contacted at renascenceatsandyport@gmail.com **or call (242)327-8719 or (301)358-0277**

Dr. Timothy Barrett at Holistic Health Services:

#6 Montgomery Street

P.O. Box N-4077

Nassau, Bahamas

Telephone: (242)325-7000 / (242)325-7003

HELP RESOURCES

Public Organizations: Local

Community Counseling & Assessment Centre (CCAC)

Bahamas Crisis Center:

East Street & Sands Road

P.O. BOX EE-17910

Nassau, Bahamas

Telephone: (242)328-0922 / (242)328-7824

Or visit: www.bahamascrisiscentre.org

Department of Social Services:

Sunshine Plaza, Blue Hill Road

P.O Box N-1545

Nassau, Bahamas

Telephone : (242)604-4200

Or visit: www.bahamas.gov.bs/socialservices

Christian Counselling Centre:

58 Collins Avenue

P.O. Box SS-6106

Nassau, Bahamas

Telephone: (242)323-7000

Other Online resources: International

Visit www.betterhelp.com

ABOUT THE AUTHOR

I am a Registered Nurse, currently pursuing a Master's in Psychology, with plans to later obtain a Doctoral degree in the same field. I am also a Blogger, Podcaster, Female Advocate, and Life Coach. I hold a Cognitive Behavioral Therapy & Psychology Certification. I am a first-time author and founder/owner of The FEmpowerment Organization, and Lyrik Statement Tees.

As far back as I can remember, I always had a strong desire to help people, and a keen interest in the human mind and behaviors of individuals. I am known as a strong person, a leader some may say, and I am against people being taken advantage of. In high school, I was given the name of Public Defender. This was because my high school best friend and I always felt the need to speak up on behalf of others who were unable to speak for themselves. That trait followed me, which resulted in me becoming the spokesperson for many things. I cannot say my approach was as refined back then as it is now, but it took some years to shape this natural-born ability.

I was awarded the resilience award in college. It was something newly done that year at the Annual Nurses Pinning Ceremony. By definition, it meant that I was a person who was able to withstand or recover quickly from difficult situations. By experience, it meant, that things happened to me in life that made me realize being strong was the only choice I've ever had.

It was when I had reached the darkest place in my life that I realized that I had not been buried but God planted me. My past shaped and aligned my purpose and developed my inclination to leave an impact on this world. It didn't hit me until the age of 30 that God had been preparing me; everything that I went through wasn't for me but it was to help someone else who couldn't do it for themselves. I am living proof that hurt people don't have to hurt people but can empower people instead.

Made in the USA
Columbia, SC
20 March 2024

33111697R00062